Alder
Apple
Ash
Beech
Birch
Blackthorn
Cherry
Horse Chestnut
Sweet Chestnut
Elm
Elder
Hazel
Hawthorn
Linden
Maple
Oak
Pine
Rowan
Sycamore
Willow
Yew

Alder

Goldfinch enjoy feasting on Alder cones

Apple

Apple trees attract insects and hedgehogs who feed off the insects and fallen apples

Ash

Bullfinch feed on winged samaras (Ash keys)

Beech

Dormice like to feed on Beech nuts

Birch

Fly agaric
mushroom
(commonly found
growing beneath
birch)

Blackthorn

Brown hairstreak butterflies
lay eggs on Blackthorn shoots

Cherry

Windfallen fruits
such as cherries are
enjoyed
by badgers

Horse Chestnut

Although poisonous to most creatures,
deer safely eat horse chestnuts

Sweet Chestnut

Chestnuts are enjoyed by wild boar

Elder

Voles enjoy eating
Elderberries and flowers

Elderflower cordial

Elm
(English)

Caterpillars of the declining white letter hairstreak butterfly feed on elms

Chaffinch like to feed off Elm seeds

Hawthorn

Hawthorn berries provide food for many birds including Robins

Hazel

As well as providing an abundance of
vitamins & minerals,
the gnawing on Hazelnuts
by squirrels helps sharpen their teeth

Female flower

Linden (Lime)

Linden flowers are
adored by bees

Maple

Maple syrup is produced by
boiling the sap drained from a hole
drilled into the tree, by a process called tapping

Oak

Squirrels use their incisors
To shell the Acorn & extract the
Inner kernel

Oak Galls formed by
tiny wasp larvae

Pine
(Scots pine)

Crossbill is a
conifer bird
specialising in prising
out pine nuts

Rowan

Rowan berries are a favourite
of the thrush and the blackbird

Sycamore

Sycamore is attractive to Ladybirds due to their diet of aphids that like to feed on plant sap from the leaves of sycamore

Willow

Goat willow is the main food supply for the rare purple emperor butterfly

Willow Warbler

Yew

Yew berries
provide an
important food
source for
fieldfares

Printed in Great Britain
by Amazon

57041215R00016